Geronimo

History Maker Bios

Catherine A. Welch

LERNER PUBLICATIONS COMPANY • MINNEAPOLIS

To my father, brother Peter, and Uncle Frank—who all served in the New York City Fire Department

The author wishes to thank Valerie Oakley and Raymond Bouley, and the staff of the Southbury, Connecticut, library for their assistance in gathering material for this book.

Geronimo's birth date, place of birth, and spelling of his Apache name appear variously across sources. The source used for this book is Angie Debo's *Geronimo: The Man, His Time, His Place.*

Lerner Publications Company
A division of Lerner Publishing Group
241 First Avenue North
Minneapolis, MN 55401 U.S.A.

Website address: www.lernerbooks.com

Map on p. 17 by Laura Westlund
Illustrations by Tim Parlin

Library of Congress Cataloging-in-Publication Data

Welch, Catherine A.
    Geronimo / by Catherine A. Welch.
        p.   cm. — (History maker bios)
    Summary: A biography of the famous Apache warrior who fought for the right of Native Americans to live and roam freely on their homeland.
    Includes bibliographical references and index.
    ISBN: 0–8225–0698–X (lib. bdg. : alk. paper)
    1. Geronimo, 1829–1909—Juvenile literature. 2. Apache Indians—Kings and rulers—Biography—Juvenile literature. 3. Apache Indians—Wars—Juvenile literature. [1. Geronimo, 1829–1909. 2. Apache Indians—Biography. 3. Indians of North America—New Mexico—Biography.] I. Title. II. Series.
E99.A6G32773 2004
979.004'972—dc21   2003011199

Manufactured in the United States of America
1 2 3 4 5 6 – JR – 09 08 07 06 05 04

TABLE OF CONTENTS

GERONIMO (GUIYATLE)
—APACHE—

INTRODUCTION

Geronimo was a Native American—a skilled Apache warrior. He lived during a time of fighting between Mexicans and Americans. They fought over land in the Southwestern part of the United States. Apache people had been living on this land for several hundred years. But in the 1800s, the Americans won a war with the Mexicans. They claimed the Apache homeland for themselves.

Geronimo loved the land and his people. He believed Apaches had the right to live on their homeland and roam freely. He led the Apaches in many fierce battles against the settlers and soldiers. He was one of the last Apaches to give up the fight.

This is his story.

1 DANGERS OF THE APACHE LIFE

As a child, Geronimo learned that the Apache world was full of dangers. He was born in the early 1820s in Gila River country, near today's state border between Arizona and New Mexico. Geronimo's childhood name was Goyahkla, meaning "One Who Yawns."

Goyahkla learned that the nearby mountains were filled with wild animals, such as mountain lions and bobcats. And there were other dangers among the rocks and pine and in the desert.

Goyahkla belonged to the Bedonkohe band, or group. This band was part of the Chiricahua Apache tribe. The Bedonkohe were good friends with three other Chiricahua Apache bands—the Chokonen, Chihenne, and Nednai. The four bands traded and visited each other's camps, or small villages.

Goyahkla, later known as Geronimo, grew up in the desert and mountains near the Gila River in the Southwest.

But Goyahkla learned that his band did not live in peace with all people. There was not much law and order in the Southwest and Mexican frontier. And life was hard. To survive, Apaches and Mexicans often raided each other. They invaded villages and stole guns, horses, and cattle.

Some Native American tribes did not get along with each other. Even Bedonkohe warriors raided camps of weaker people. Raiding was a way of life.

The Apache people lived in tipis. Sometimes they lived in brush-covered wickiups.

Warriors, such as these three Apache men, protected their community and supplied food for their families.

Goyahkla learned that every tribe needed great warriors. Warriors carried out important raids. Warriors hunted for their families and protected the women and children. The greatest warriors became Apache leaders.

Goyahkla liked to hear about the great warriors. His father, Taklishim, told him about the battles and about the thrill of hunting. Apache history was filled with stories of war and raids.

The Apaches were hard workers. Men, women, and children each had different jobs to do.

His mother, Juana, taught him about Usen, the Apache God. He learned that Usen created the Apaches. Usen made the land full of grain, fruit, and animals to eat. Usen put healing herbs on the earth. Goyahkla learned to pray to Usen for good health, strength, wisdom, and protection.

Like other boys and girls, Goyahkla was given many chores. Apaches disliked lazy people. Children helped grow melons, pumpkins, beans, and corn. They helped keep the band's ponies and wild animals away from the crops. After harvest, they stored food in caves.

Goyahkla did not laugh often. He was a serious boy. But his tribe loved to laugh and play jokes on each other. And for special events, there was feasting, dancing, and singing. Goyahkla loved these celebrations.

When Goyahkla was seven, he began his training as a warrior. The older warriors told him that his legs were his best friends. They made him and the other boys race to the top of mountains before sunrise. They made them bathe in an icy creek and then stand in the snow. Goyahkla shivered, but he never complained.

Apaches perform a traditional dance.

With his cousins, he played war games and learned how to "creep and freeze." He learned to stay motionless for minutes—standing or crouching. He learned to dodge stones thrown by the other boys.

He also learned how to hunt. As a boy, Goyahkla practiced using his bow and arrows. He chased after wild turkeys and rabbits, killing them with a club. When he was about ten, he joined the men, chasing deer, antelope, elk, and bison that roamed the Apache land.

Apache warriors hunted herds of bison and other large animals.

A Roaming Way of Life

Apache bands were nomadic. They did not live in one place all year long. They moved from place to place each season. They moved to find more animals to hunt. They moved where wild food grew at different times of the year. Goyahkla learned to love the freedom of roaming throughout the Apache homeland. This freedom became important to him.

As Goyahkla grew older, he joined warriors on raids. Goyahkla needed to go on four raids before he could become a true warrior. As part of his training, Goyahkla also cared for the horses. At times, he got water and wood and cooked for the grown men. Sometimes, he sat up at night, guarding the camp.

Goyahkla's best friend was Juh. This boy lived with the fierce Nednai band in the Sierra Madre Mountains of Mexico.

Some boys teased Juh because he stuttered. But Goyahkla liked Juh because he was strong and had a fighting spirit.

While Goyahkla was still training to be a warrior, his father died. Following the Apache ways, his father's body was laid to rest in a cave. Goyahkla was sad to see his father die. But he took care of his mother, and he kept training to be a warrior.

2 BECOMING A WARRIOR

One day, Juana decided she and Goyahkla should visit her husband's Nednai relatives. The trip would also teach Goyahkla more about the land Apaches roamed. The Apache homeland was a large territory.

Goyahkla looked forward to visiting his good friend Juh and his cousin Ishton. Ishton had married Juh and lived with the Nednai band.

Goyahkla and his mother probably went with a small group of women, children, and warriors. They walked several hundred miles, crossing thick forest, deep canyons, and snow-covered mountains. They watched for Mexicans, who wanted Apaches killed.

Apaches were skilled travelers. This group is crossing the Gila River.

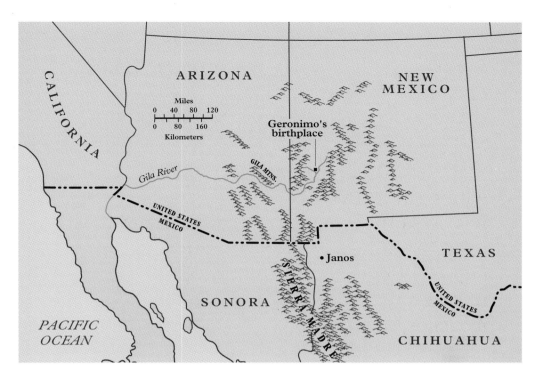

While Goyahkla was growing up, some Apaches had killed thousands of Mexican settlers in different raids. By 1837, the Mexican states of Sonora and Chihuahua had passed a law. They paid money for every Apache warrior, woman, or child that was killed.

At night, Goyahkla and the other travelers crossed the open flatland. During the day, they hid in the mountain brush. Goyahkla learned how Apaches covered their tracks and hid their camps.

He also learned what to do if Mexicans attacked. Everyone was to scatter and hide. When it was safe, they would meet at a certain spot. The trip taught him important lessons about how to travel safely—the Apache way.

When he was about seventeen, he became a warrior. Goyahkla couldn't wait to serve his people. He also wanted to begin a family. As a warrior, he could marry. He had his eye on one slender girl, Alope, in the Nednai band.

Alope became Goyahkla's wife. They lived in a tipi covered with buffalo skins. Alope drew pictures on the tanned hides. She made decorations with beads. They had three children and were happy for many years.

While Goyahkla enjoyed his life with Alope, a war began. The United States and Mexico were fighting over land in the Southwest. In 1848, the war ended. Land in today's states of New Mexico and Arizona became part of the United States. The United States promised to stop Apaches from raiding in Mexico.

The Mexican War was fought from 1846 to 1848.

Some Mexicans wanted to make peace with Apaches. The Mexican state of Chihuahua invited Apache people to trade in their towns. If Apaches got supplies by trading, then maybe they would not need to raid Mexican towns. Apaches could trade animal hides and furs for cloth, knives, and ornaments.

In about 1850, Goyahkla's Bedonkohe band went to Chihuahua to trade. The women and children camped outside the town of Janos. A few warriors guarded them. Goyahkla and the other men went into Janos to trade.

In Chihuahua, Apache goods, such as woven baskets, could be traded for desirable Mexican items.

Goyahkla and other Apache warriors return to camp after a day of trading in Janos.

At the same time, four hundred Mexican soldiers marched toward Janos. The soldiers were from the Mexican state of Sonora. They believed some Apaches had stolen seven mules from a town in Sonora. The Sonoran soldiers were not interested in making peace.

The Mexican soldiers stormed into the Apache camp. They took ponies, guns, and supplies. They killed and captured many Apaches. A few women and children escaped. They met Goyahkla and the other warriors heading back to camp. They told the warriors what had happened.

Fearing the soldiers would attack them, the Apaches scattered and hid. At night, they gathered at the meeting place—a spot of thick bushes.

Goyahkla's loss was the greatest. His whole family was dead—mother, wife, and three children. He was shocked. He stood alone by the river. His sadness was so deep, he could not speak.

Later, the eighty remaining warriors met to talk about the killings. Goyahkla took his place in the meeting circle. But still, he could not speak.

WARRIORS AND WIVES

Apache women needed husbands to hunt animals and bring supplies back from raids. But men were often killed in raids or battles. During times of war, warriors often had more than one wife. That way no woman was left alone. Goyahkla married another woman a few months after Alope was killed.

Eighty warriors could not fight an army of four hundred soldiers. Chief Mangas Coloradas ordered everyone to quickly and quietly go back to Arizona. They could not get the bodies of the dead and bury them. They must leave before the Mexicans attacked and killed them.

Goyahkla was the last to leave. He knew the vultures and coyotes would eat the bodies of his loved ones. This made his sadness and loss even greater.

3 FIGHTING BACK

When Goyahkla returned to his tipi, he looked at Alope's decorations. He looked at his children's playthings. He was heartbroken. He burned everything, even his tipi.

He felt that he would never be happy again. His deep sadness turned into deep anger against the Mexicans. He wanted to kill them.

One day while crying, he heard a voice. It called his name, "Goyahkla." It told him that no guns would ever kill him. He would never be killed in battle.

The voice called his name four times. For Apaches, four was a magical number. Goyahkla believed the voice. He believed he now had a special power.

MEDICINE MAN

Goyahkla was a famous medicine man. Medicine men and women treated wounds and cured the sick. When healing people, he sang songs, beat a drum, and prayed.

Apaches believed other powers came suddenly to Goyahkla during the years. One power let him know what was going to happen before it happened. Sometimes he knew when soldiers were coming, and he warned his people. Apaches also thought Goyahkla had the power to make it rain or storm.

The other warriors also wanted to battle the Mexicans. They had lost loved ones too. They believed the life of an Apache was worth many dead Mexicans. Chief Mangas Coloradas and the warriors planned an attack. Goyahkla wanted to help.

He visited Chief Cochise of the Chokonen band. He also talked to Juh, now chief of the Nednai. He wanted their warriors to join the attack. "I will fight in front of the battle," Goyahkla promised them. The other bands agreed to fight. They would show the Mexicans how much Apaches loved their own people.

Chief Cochise became a respected and well-known Apache leader.

Goyahkla had become an angry and powerful warrior.

Almost a year after Goyahkla's family was killed, the Apaches prepared for battle. First, they hid their families in the mountains with a guard. Then the warriors painted their faces and put on war bands. War paint made it easier to tell their own people apart from the enemy.

The warriors walked fourteen hours a day until they reached Mexico. Goyahkla was not a chief. But the other warriors gave him the honor of leading the battle.

Geronimo leads a group of Apache warriors.

As the battle began, Goyahkla thought of his mother, wife, and children. For two hours, he and the other Apache warriors fought fiercely. Many Apaches and Mexicans were killed.

It is believed that Goyahkla got his name "Geronimo" during this battle. He did not fear the soldiers' bullets. He fought wildly with his hunting knife. The soldiers were terrified. They cried out "Geronimo," Spanish for Saint Jerome. They called to Saint Jerome for help.

Months later, Geronimo went to Mexico with small groups of warriors—sometimes twenty-five or more. The Apaches attacked Mexican villages for supplies. Often the Mexicans fled in horror as soon as they heard the Apaches coming.

Geronimo and his men took blankets, calico fabric, saddles, tinware, and sugar. If they captured cattle, they often drove these home by foot to their families. The supplies would keep their families alive during the winter.

Sometimes Mexican troops hunted down Geronimo and the other warriors. They tried to stop the Apache raids. Mexican soldiers found Apache camps and burned tipis. They killed women, children, and warriors. Geronimo was injured in several battles. But he had the courage to keep fighting. He believed his special power would keep him alive.

4 CHASING GERONIMO

During the 1850s, Geronimo continued raiding Mexican villages. He also met white Americans for the first time. Some of these American men came to trap animals for their valuable furs. The Apaches did not mind them.

But then the miners came. These men searched for gold beneath the land. Geronimo saw them dig up the earth. He watched them dirty the water.

Geronimo began to think the Americans were no better than the Mexicans. The Americans were greedy. They wanted gold, horses, and cattle. They killed or scared off animals the Apaches hunted for food. The white men wanted everything that was on the Apache homeland.

One day Chief Mangas Coloradas went to the miners' camp. He wanted the miners to leave the Apache land. He planned to tell them of a different place they could find gold. But the miners tied up the chief and whipped him.

American miners came to the Apache homeland in search of gold.

Mangas survived, but Geronimo and the other warriors were outraged. Then soldiers falsely accused Chief Cochise of taking a boy. They killed a few of Cochise's relatives. This event further angered the Apaches. Mangas, Cochise, and Geronimo led attacks against white settlers. Then the U.S. government sent soldiers to battle the Apache warriors. Many people died.

DESERT WARS

Geronimo and the other Apache warriors knew how to hide themselves from soldiers in the desert. They rubbed their bodies with clay and sand to blend in with their surroundings. They traveled quickly and quietly by foot and carried no supplies. They knew where to find wild honey, berries, cactus fruit, and water holes.

American soldiers traveled slowly, with wagonloads of supplies. And the hot desert drove them crazy with thirst.

Geronimo was unhappy with the frontier towns that sprang up on the Apache homeland.

Each year, Geronimo saw more wagons come with settlers. He saw ranches and frontier towns spring up. He saw houses and fences. Soon the herds of deer were fewer. There was less meat to eat and less land to roam.

More than ever, the warriors felt they needed to raid and steal in order to survive. They struck ranches and attacked stagecoaches. They killed farmers and cowboys. They also continued to battle with American soldiers. Geronimo and the other warriors would fiercely protect their land and families.

An Apache reservation

By 1870, President Ulysses S. Grant wanted to end the warfare in the Southwest. The settlers wanted to live and work in peace. But the settlers also wanted the best land for themselves.

The U.S. government began forcing all Native Americans onto land called reservations. This was land settlers did not want. It was often too dry for growing crops. The U.S. government promised Native Americans food, training and tools to farm, and other supplies. But those promises were often broken.

By this time, Geronimo was almost fifty years old. He lived on the reservations at times. But he did not stay for long. He wanted the freedom to roam and hunt.

Several times, Geronimo escaped from the reservation, taking a band of Apaches with him. At one point, he joined Chief Juh at a secret camp in the Sierra Madre Mountains in Mexico. Together, they raided the Mexican settlements for supplies. They also battled with Americans who wanted to put them in prison or kill them. Geronimo used all his Apache skills to protect himself and the others.

This famous portrait of Geronimo shows his determination to fight for the Apache people.

After years of fighting, many Apaches became weary. They wanted peace. They stayed on the reservations and tried to accept their new way of life. But Geronimo kept fighting. He still wanted his freedom, the Apache land, and the Apache way of life.

Geronimo became a famous symbol. To some Native Americans, he was a hero who would never stop fighting for justice. To white Americans, he was feared and hated. The Americans wanted to capture him for good.

This group of men and women lived in hiding with Geronimo away from the reservations.

Geronimo, (SECOND FROM LEFT) and George Crook, (SECOND FROM RIGHT) met to talk about Geronimo's surrender.

In 1882, an American general named George Crook discovered Juh's hideout and tracked down Geronimo. But Geronimo got away. Then sometime in 1883, Juh tumbled to his death when his horse fell off a steep slope.

Geronimo was shocked at the loss of his fierce friend. In 1884, he surrendered to General Crook and returned to the reservation. But a year later, he fled once again.

Things quickly got worse. General Nelson A. Miles sent thousands of troops to capture Geronimo. Soldiers kept Geronimo and his men on the run. The warriors could never sleep at night. At the slightest sound, they jumped up and grabbed their weapons.

Finally, Geronimo and the warriors no longer had the will to fight. They wanted to return to their families on the reservation. They saw that thousands of settlers now lived on Apache land. The Southern Pacific Railroad ran through it. Geronimo knew the old way of life was gone forever.

5 PRISONERS OF WAR

Geronimo spoke with General Miles about making peace. Miles said Geronimo's past crimes would be forgiven if he surrendered. Miles used friendly words to win over Geronimo. Miles said the new Florida reservation was a good place with lots of trees and animals to hunt. He said Geronimo's wife, children, and all his people were on that reservation.

Geronimo (FRONT ROW, THIRD FROM RIGHT) *with other captured Apache warriors*

On September 4, 1886, Geronimo surrendered to Miles. But the friendly General Miles did not keep his promises. He put Geronimo and the warriors on a train. He shipped them to a prison in Florida known as Fort Pickens.

The Apache prisoners worked every day. Geronimo sawed large logs. The men did not see their families, who were in St. Augustine, Florida. Many Apaches got sick and died. The white man's diseases were killing them. Apaches were far from the healing plants and herbs of their homeland.

The prisoners were sent from one prison camp to the next. Each one was just as bad as the other. By 1894, the Apaches were moved to a prison called Fort Sill in Oklahoma.

The warriors were now with their families. Life was a little better there. Houses were built for the Apaches. They were given cattle, hogs, turkeys, and chickens. They were taught how to farm. But Geronimo still missed his old way of life.

GERONIMO THE SHOWMAN

Geronimo became a famous Apache warrior. People wanted to see how he looked and talked. They wanted to hear about his life. He became an attraction at special events, such as the 1904 World's Fair in St. Louis, Missouri. Sometimes he entered roping contests in the Wild West shows. Wherever Geronimo went, he asked people to let him return to his Arizona homeland.

In March 1905, President Theodore Roosevelt invited Geronimo to Washington, D.C. Roosevelt was starting his second term as president. He thought the famous Apache warrior would add excitement to his inaugural celebration.

In Washington, D.C., Geronimo begged Roosevelt to send the Apaches back to Arizona. But the president said that people in Arizona and New Mexico hated and feared the Apaches. If the Apaches went back, there would be more bloodshed.

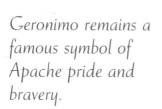

Geronimo remains a famous symbol of Apache pride and bravery.

Geronimo wanted to spend his last days in Arizona and be buried in the mountains there. But he did not get his wish. He died on February 17, 1909, and was buried in a graveyard at Fort Sill. He was about eighty-six years old.

Geronimo and his people killed many Mexican and American people. But Mexicans and Americans also killed many Apache men, women, and children. Geronimo's fight for his Apache homeland is an important part of American history. In his own way, he fought for freedom and justice.

TIMELINE

In the year . . .

1830 Geronimo began his training as a warrior. Age 7

1840 he became a warrior and married Alope.

1848 the United States won the war against Mexico. The U.S. government claimed the Spanish Southwest, which included part of the Apache homeland.

1850 his mother, wife, and three children were killed by Mexicans in the city of Janos. Age 27

1851 he went to battle against Mexicans.
he met white Americans for the first time.

1861 he joined Chief Cochise and other Apaches in warfare against American soldiers. Age 38

1870 the U.S. government began forcing Apaches onto reservations.

1881 he led one of several breakouts from an Apache reservation.

1882 he was tracked down by General George Crook Age 59

1884 he made his first surrender to General Crook.

1885 he fled the reservation for the last time.

1886 he surrendered to General Nelson A. Miles, ending warfare between the Apache and white settlers. Age 63

1894 he and his people were moved to Fort Sill, Oklahoma. Age 71

1904 he appeared at the St. Louis World's Fair. Age 81

1905 he rode in President Theodore Roosevelt's inaugural parade.
he told his life story to Stephen M. Barrett.

1909 he died at Fort Sill. Age 86

44

THE VICTORY CRY

Geronimo was not forgotten after he died. The country remembered him and the Apaches who fought with him. Apaches are remembered as brave and skillful warriors.

During World War II, American soldiers shouted Geronimo's name for courage. They used his name whenever they had to jump from planes. With parachutes strapped to their backs, they cried, "Geronimo!" Then they leaped from the planes into the sky. Years later, the U.S. Army nicknamed a famous type of fighter helicopter the Apache.

FURTHER READING

NONFICTION

Hoyt-Goldsmith, Diane. *Apache Rodeo.* New York: Holiday House, 1995. An Apache girl named Felicita describes modern life for Apache children, including the yearly rodeo held in her hometown of Whitewater, Arizona.

Moskal, Greg. *An Apache Indian Community.* New York: Powerkids Press, 2002. Moskal describes life for the children and adults living together in an Apache community.

Netzley, Patricia. *Apache Warriors.* San Diego: Kidhaven Press, 2002. Part of the Daily Life series, this book explores life for Apache warriors in the American Southwest during the 1800s.

Santella, Andrew. *The Apache.* New York: Children's Press, 2001. An introduction to the Apache culture, traditions, history, and modern-day life.

Sita, Lisa. *Coming of Age.* Woodbridge, CT: Blackbirch Press, 1999. Describes the coming-of-age rituals practiced by a number of world cultures, including the Apache people.

FICTION

Lacapa, Michael. *The Flute Player: An Apache Folktale.* Flagstaff, AZ: Rising Moon, 1990. Lacapa, a man of Apache and Hopi descent, tells the ancient Apache folktale of a flute player who made music that sounded like wind in a canyon.

McKissack, Patricia C. *Run Away Home.* New York: Scholastic, 1997. In 1886, in Alabama, an eleven-year-old African American girl and her family learn of the Apache fighters being taken to prison. They befriend and give refuge to one Apache boy who has managed to run away.

WEBSITES

The Chiricahua-Warm Springs-Fort Sill Apache Tribe of Oklahoma Official Website
<http://fsat.tripod.com> This website is filled with information about Geronimo's Apache band.

Geronimo: His Own Story
<http://odur.let.rug.nl/~usa/B/geronimo/geronixx.htm> Geronimo's story, as told to S. M. Barrett, is available on this website.

SELECT BIBLIOGRAPHY

Adams, Alexander B. *Geronimo: A Biography.* New York: G.P. Putnam's Sons, 1971.

Aleshire, Peter. *The Fox and the Whirlwind: General George Crook and Geronimo.* New York: John Wiley & Sons, Inc., 2000.

Barrett, S. M., ed. Geronimo's Story of His Life. 1906. Reprint. New York: Irvington Publishers, Inc., 1983.

Betzinez, Jason, and Wilbur Sturtevant Nye. *I Fought with Geronimo.* Harrisburg, PA: The Stackpole Company, 1960.

Debo, Angie. *Geronimo: The Man, His Time, His Place.* Norman, OK: University of Oklahoma Press, 1976.

Haley, James L. *Apaches, a History and Culture Portrait.* Garden City, NY: Doubleday, 1981.

Roberts, David. *Once They Moved Like the Wind: Cochise, Geronimo, and the Apache Wars.* New York: Simon & Schuster, 1993.

INDEX

Acknowledgments

For photographs and artwork: Library of Congress, LC-USZ62-124560, p. 4; © Northwind Picture Archives, p. 7; Library of Congress, LC-USZ62-104919, p. 8; Library of Congress, LC-USZ62-104711, p. 9; American Museum of Natural History, p. 10; Library of Congress, LC-USZ62-112201, p. 11; © Jim Simondet/ Independent Picture Service, p. 12; Arizona Historical Society, Tucson, pp. 16, 28; Library of Congress, LC-USZ62-115465, p. 18; Library of Congress, pp. 19, 20; Library of Congress, LC-USZ62-117474, p. 21; Arizona Historical Society, p. 26; Western History Collection, University of Oklahoma Library, pp. 27, 36, 37; South Dakota Historical Society – State Archives, pp. 31, 33; Library of Congress, LC-USZC4-5661, p. 34; Smithsonian Institution National Anthropological Archives, Bureau of American Ethnology Collection, pp. 35, 40; Library of Congress, LC-USZ62-83557, p. 42; Bettmann/CORBIS, p. 45. Front cover, Western History Collection, University of Oklahoma Library. Back cover, Library of Congress.